ALFRED'S B
ROCK GUITAR METHOD 1

MW01076729

THE MOST POPULAR SERIES FOR LEARNING HOW TO PLAY
For individual or class instruction

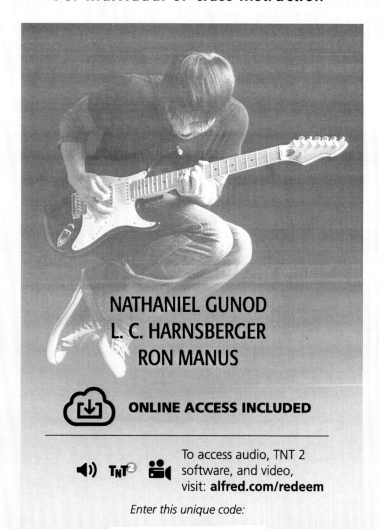

NATHANIEL GUNOD
L. C. HARNSBERGER
RON MANUS

PLAY LOUD

 ONLINE ACCESS INCLUDED

🔊 TNT2 🎥 To access audio, TNT 2 software, and video, visit: **alfred.com/redeem**

Enter this unique code:

00-45052_54535074

Alfred

alfred.com

Book & Online Video/Audio/Software
ISBN-10: 1-4706-3231-4
ISBN-13: 978-1-4706-3231-1

Back cover photo models: Janet Robin (top), janetrobin.com • Paris Carney (middle left), pariscarney.com • Luis Cabezas from The Dollyrots (middle right), thedollyrots.com
Back cover photos: Top three photos: Kevin Estrada • Bottom photo: © Wolfgang Lienbacher / Vetta / Getty Images
Audio performed by Jared Meeker • All accompaniment arrangements by Jared Meeker except "Good Times Bad Times," arranged by Mark Burgess.

Contents

The Parts of Your Guitar

The Acoustic Guitar

The Electric Guitar

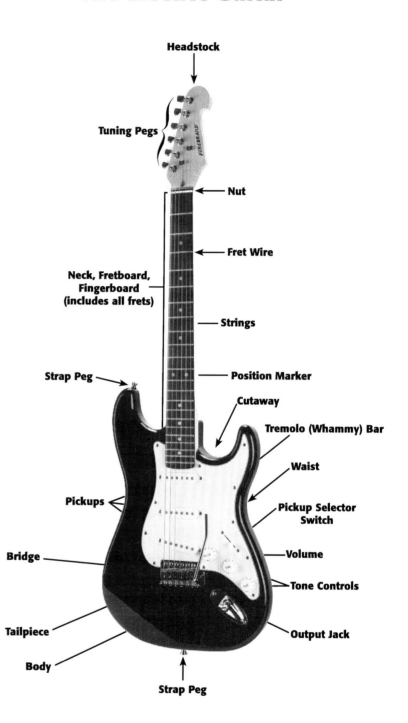

The Acoustic Guitar

- Headstock
- Tuning Pegs
- Nut
- Strings
- Neck, Fretboard, Fingerboard (includes all frets)
- Fret Wire
- Position Marker
- Soundhole
- Waist
- Bridge
- Body

The Electric Guitar

- Headstock
- Tuning Pegs
- Nut
- Fret Wire
- Neck, Fretboard, Fingerboard (includes all frets)
- Strings
- Position Marker
- Strap Peg
- Cutaway
- Tremolo (Whammy) Bar
- Waist
- Pickups
- Pickup Selector Switch
- Bridge
- Volume
- Tone Controls
- Output Jack
- Tailpiece
- Body
- Strap Peg

Which Guitar Is Best for Me?

Which guitar is the "right" guitar for you? It's all a matter of taste, what kind of music you want to play, and what you want to sound like. Some beginners say a nylon-string guitar is easier on their fingers, but eventually you're going to get calluses and become accustomed to any guitar you practice on. The most important consideration is probably the size: if you have small hands, you will find a smaller guitar easier to play. Also, a guitar with a very big, fat body will be hard for a small person to manage. It's just common sense. If you want to rock out, it's perfectly fine to start learning on an electric guitar—there are no rules about which guitar to get first. Get one that you will want to pick up and play every day!

How to Hold Your Guitar

Hold your guitar in a position that is most comfortable for you. Some positions are shown below .

When playing, keep your left wrist away from the fingerboard. This will allow your fingers to be in a better position to finger the chords. Press your fingers firmly, but make sure they do not touch the neighboring strings.

Tilt the neck slightly up. Don't twist the body of the guitar to see the strings better.

Standing with strap.

Sitting.

Sitting with legs crossed.

The Amplifier

If you are playing an electric guitar, you will need to use an *amplifier*. The amplifier (or amp) makes the sound of a guitar louder, and allows you to add effects to your sound like distortion. All amps are different, but here are a few features you will find on virtually every amp.

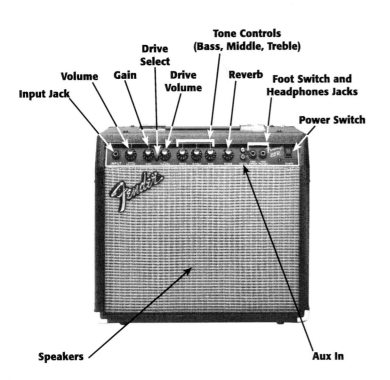

Aux In: RCA input jacks for use with a portable CD or tape player, drum machine, etc.

Input jacks: This is where you plug in your guitar with a ¼" plug.

Drive Select: Activates the Drive channel.

Drive Volume: Controls the loudness of the Drive channel.

Foot Switch and Headphones Jacks: Plug in your optional foot switch for changing channels, or your mono or stereo headphones.

Gain: This control, sometimes called "drive," will adjust the amount of effects, such as distortion, added to your sound.

Power Switch: This switch turns the unit ON and OFF.

Reverb: Reverb adds an echo sound to your playing. Not all amps have this feature.

Speakers: The sound comes directly out of the amp through the speakers. Be careful not to touch the speakers because they are easily damaged.

Tone Controls: You can adjust the high (treble), middle, and low (bass) sounds of your guitar. Adjust these controls to find a sound you like.

Volume: The higher the number, the louder the sound. Be aware of who is around you before turning up the volume.

The Right Hand

Strumming with a Pick

Hold the pick between your thumb and index finger. Grip it firmly, but don't squeeze too hard.

Strum from the 6th string (the thickest, lowest-sounding string) to the 1st string (the thinnest, highest-sounding string).

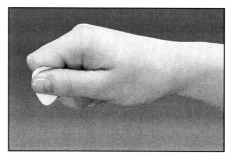

Correct way to hold a pick.

Important: Strum by mostly moving your wrist, not just your arm. Use as little motion as possible. Start as close to the top string as you can, and never let your hand move past the edge of the guitar.

Start near the top string.

Move mostly your wrist, not just your arm. Finish near the bottom string.

The Left Hand

Proper Left-Hand Position

Learning to use your left-hand fingers starts with a good hand position. Place your hand so your thumb rests comfortably in the middle of the back of the neck. Position your fingers on the strings as if you are gently squeezing a ball between them and your thumb. Keep your elbow in and your fingers curved.

Keep your elbow in and fingers curved. Arch your wrist slightly so your fingertips can more easily come down on top of the strings.

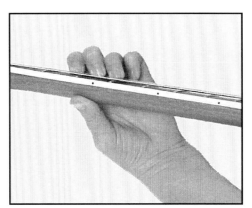

Position fingers as if you are gently squeezing a ball between your fingertips and thumb. Place the thumb behind the fingerboard opposite the 2nd finger.

Placing a Finger on a String

When you press a string with a left-hand finger, make sure you press firmly with the tip of your finger and as close to the fret wire as you can without actually being right on it. Short fingernails are important! This will create a clean, bright tone.

Right!
Finger presses the string down near the fret without actually being on it.

Wrong!
Finger is too far from the fret wire; the tone is "buzzy" and indefinite.

Wrong!
Finger is on top of the fret wire; the tone is muffled and unclear.

How to Tune Your Guitar

First, make sure your strings are wound properly around the tuning pegs. They should go from the inside to the outside as illustrated to the right. Some guitars have all six tuning pegs on the same side of the headstock. If this is the case, make sure all six strings are wound the same way, from the inside out.

Turning a tuning peg clockwise makes the string looser and the pitch lower. Turning a tuning peg counterclockwise makes the string tighter and the pitch higher. Be sure not to tighten the strings too much because they could break. Always pluck the string and listen as you turn the tuning pegs.

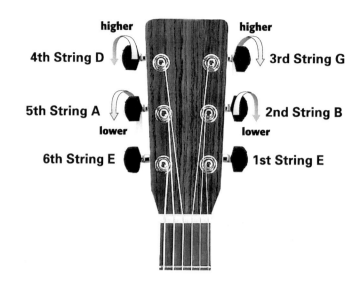

Important

Always remember that the thinnest, highest-sounding string, the one closest to the floor, is the 1st string. The thickest, lowest-sounding string, the one closest to the ceiling, is the 6th string. When guitarists say "the highest string," they are referring to the highest-sounding string.

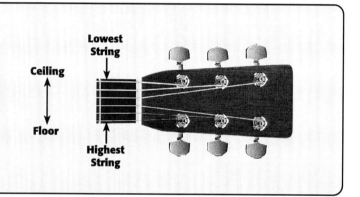

Tuning the Guitar to Itself

Tune the 6th string to E on the keyboard. If no keyboard is available, approximate E as best as you can and proceed as follows:

Press 5th fret of 6th string to get pitch of 5th string (A).

Press 5th fret of 5th string to get pitch of 4th string (D).

Press 5th fret of 4th string to get pitch of 3rd string (G).

Press 4th fret of 3rd string to get pitch of 2nd string (B).

Press 5th fret of 2nd string to get pitch of 1st string (E).

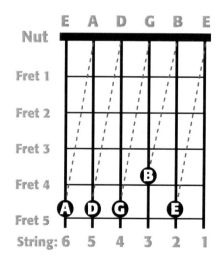

Tuning with the Online Audio

 Track 1

To tune while listening to the online audio, listen to the directions and match each of your strings to the corresponding pitches.

How to Use an Electronic Tuner

An electronic tuner is a handy device that can help keep your guitar in tune. You pick each string one at a time, and the tuner guides you to the exact pitch the string should be in order for it to be in tune. Until your ear becomes more experienced, an electronic tuner can be extremely useful.

Getting Acquainted with Music

Musical sounds are indicated by symbols called *notes*. Their time value is determined by their color (white or black) and by *stems* or *flags* attached to the *note head*.

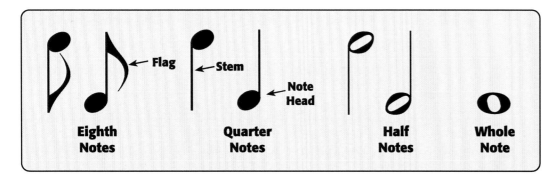

The Staff

The notes are named after the first seven letters of the alphabet (A–G), endlessly repeated to embrace the entire range of musical sound. The name and pitch of the note is determined by its position on five horizontal lines and the spaces between, called the *staff*.

5th LINE

4th LINE   4th SPACE

3rd LINE   3rd SPACE

2nd LINE   2nd SPACE

1st LINE   1st SPACE

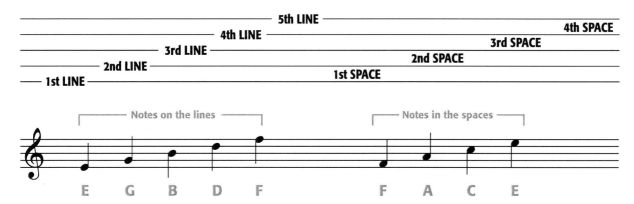

Notes on the lines   Notes in the spaces

E G B D F   F A C E

Measures

Music is divided into equal parts called *measures*, or *bars*. One measure is divided from another by a *bar line*.

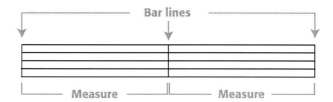

Bar lines

Measure   Measure

Clefs

During the evolution of musical notation, the staff had from 2 to 20 lines, and symbols were invented to locate certain lines and the pitch of the note on that line. These symbols are called *clefs*. Music for guitar is written in the *G clef*, or *treble clef*.

G

How to Read Chord Diagrams

Fingering diagrams show where to place the fingers of your left hand. Strings not played are shown with dashed lines and an X. The number within the circle indicates the finger that is pressed down.

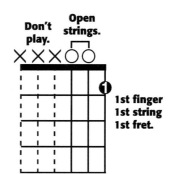

Don't play.

Open strings.

1st finger
1st string
1st fret.

Left-Hand Finger Numbers

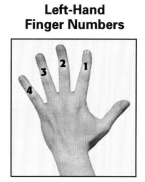

The Sixth String E Track 2

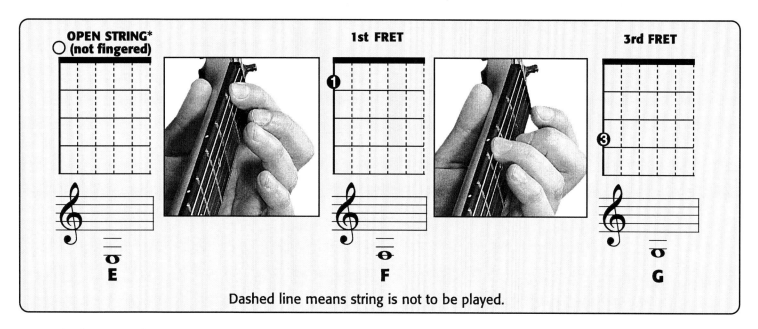

Dashed line means string is not to be played.

Use only down-strokes, indicated by ⊓. The symbol ○ under or over a note means *open string.* Do not finger.

It is easy to tell the notes E, F, and G apart. E is the note under the three lines below the staff. F is on the third line below the staff. G is under the two lines below the staff.

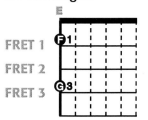

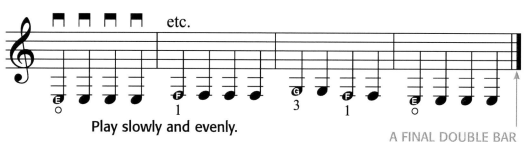

Play slowly and evenly.

A FINAL DOUBLE BAR SHOWS THE END OF AN EXAMPLE OR SONG.

SIXTH-STRING RIFF 1 Track 3

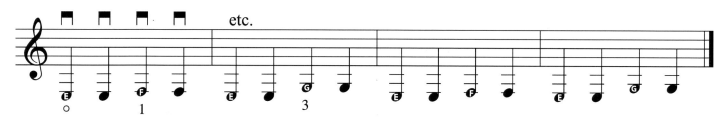

A *riff* is a short, repeated melodic pattern.

SIXTH-STRING RIFF 2  Track 4

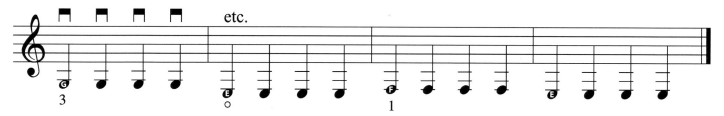

*Though no photo is shown for the open string, the fingers of the left hand should remain slightly above the string, ready to play the correct fret when needed. The thumb should also remain in its proper position.

10

More Riffs 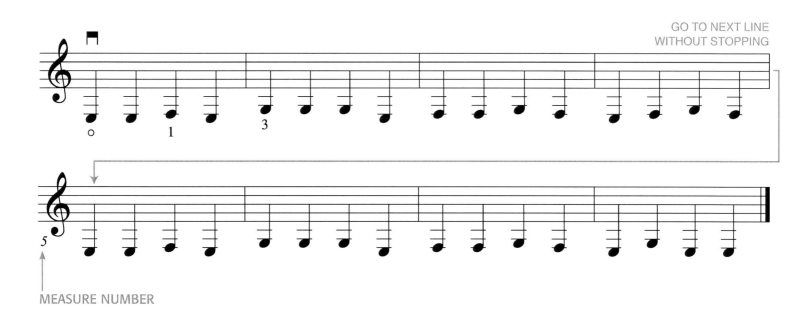 Track 5

Still More Riffs Track 6

ROCKIN' BASS LINE Track 7

Silent Guitar Calisthenics 1 and 2

This exercise is silent because it is done with the left hand alone. The goal is to go as slowly as possible, keeping one finger down on the string as you add the other, and pressing the string down more firmly than usual. You are working on the muscles that spread the fingers apart, and this will help develop your reach. Use the left side of the tip of your 1st finger and the exact middle of the tip of your 3rd finger. Remember to place the fingers just to the left of the frets.

When both fingers are down they should look similar to this.

Sound-Off: How to Count Time

Four Kinds of Notes

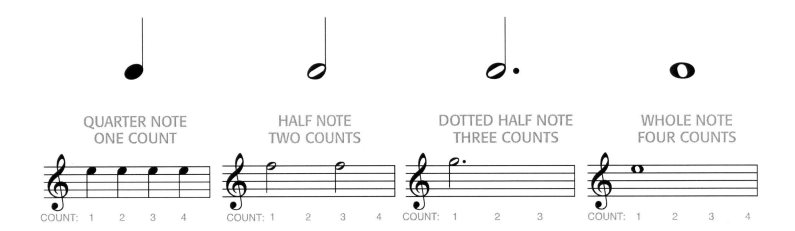

Time Signatures

Each piece of music has numbers at the beginning called a *time signature*.
These numbers tell us how to count time.

The TOP NUMBER tells us how many counts are in each measure.
The BOTTOM NUMBER tells us what kind of note gets one count.

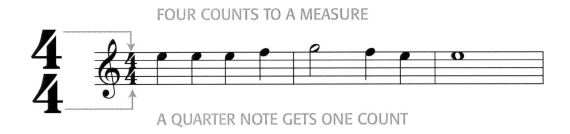

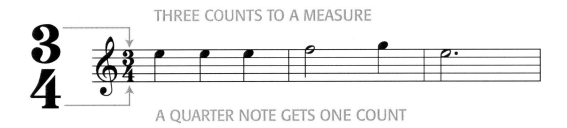

Important: Go back and fill in the missing time signatures of the songs you have already learned.

The Fifth String A 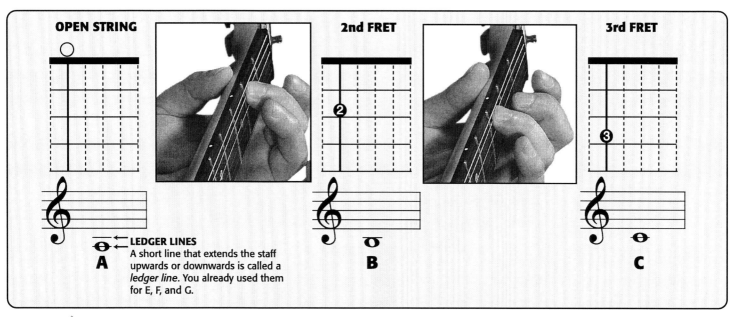 Track 8

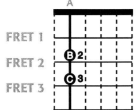

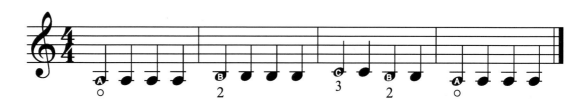

JAMMING ON 5 AND 6 Track 9

TWO-STRING ROCK Track 10

14

Easy Rock Riffs on the 5th and 6th Strings

Repeat Signs

The double dots inside the double bars are *repeat signs*, and they indicate that everything between the double bars must be repeated.

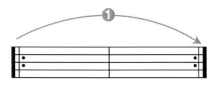 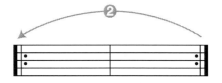 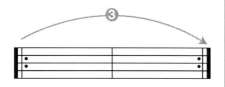

KING LOUIE Track 11

The following example is in the style of The Kingsmen's major hit, "Louie Louie."

AS I ARRIVE Track 12

This one's in the style of the classic Green Day song "When I Come Around."

FERROUS GUY  Track 13

The riff below is in the style of "Iron Man" by Black Sabbath.

THEY CAN ROCK  Track 14

This is in the style of Queen's huge hit "We Will Rock You."

Silent Guitar Calisthenics 3

As with the calisthenics on page 11, this exercise is silent because it is done with the left hand alone. Do this as slowly as possible, keeping one finger down on the string as you add the other, and pressing the string down more firmly than usual. This time, concentrate on lifting one finger as far away as you can while pressing down firmly with the other. This will help you develop some independence between your 2nd and 3rd fingers. Remember to place the fingers just to the left of the frets.

When both fingers are down, they should look similar to this.

Hold down 2nd finger	Lift 2nd finger high	(Place 2nd finger firmly on 2nd fret)	Lift 3rd finger high

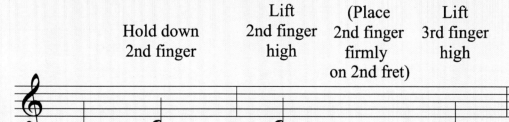

The Fourth String D Track 15

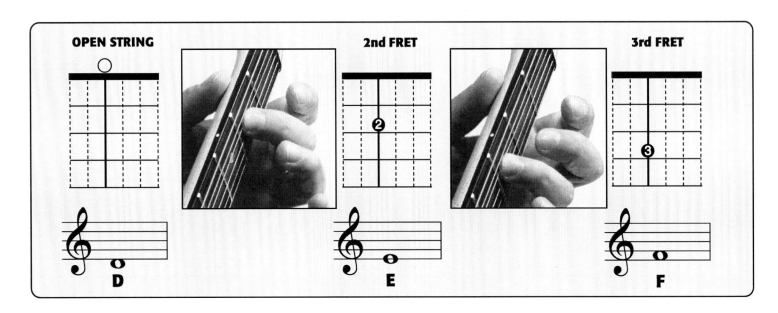

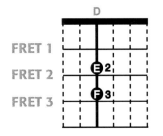

Fourth-String Riff Track 16

1950s Rock Lick Track 17

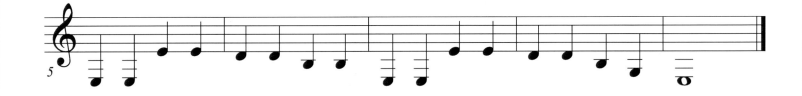

FOGGY LAKE  Track 18

This next example is in the style of "Smoke on the Water" by the group Deep Purple.

LADDER TO THE SKY  Track 19

The example below is in the style of one of the most popular rock songs ever,
"Stairway to Heaven" by Led Zeppelin.

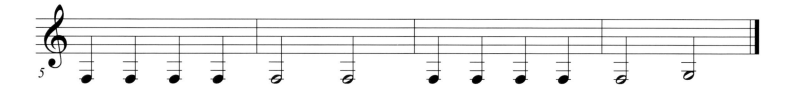

CRAZY KID  Track 20

This example is in the style of "Wild Child" by The Doors.

Playing Two Notes Together Track 21

Until now, you have been playing one note at a time, but in the next example, you will play two notes at once. Make sure to pick the notes quickly so they produce one sound and do not have the effect of two separate notes.

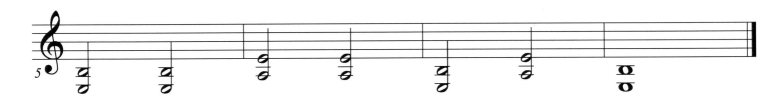

BLUES IN 3 Track 22

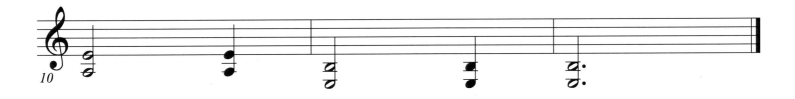

The Third String G  Track 23

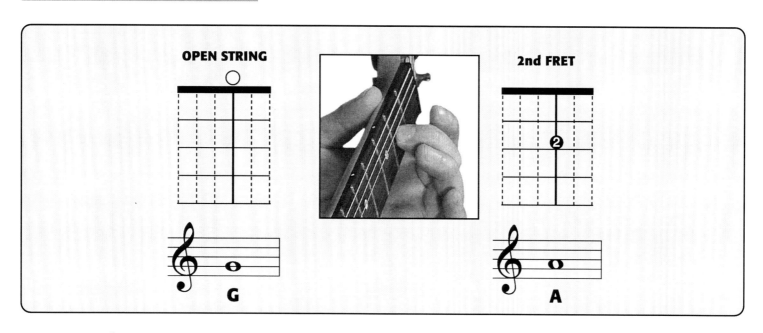

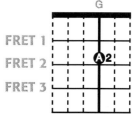

CASH  Track 24

This example is in the style of "Money" by The Beatles.

Quarter Rest

This sign indicates silence for one count. For a clearer effect, you may stop the sound of the strings by touching the strings lightly with the heel of the right hand.

ODE TO JOY Track 25

Before Led Zeppelin was formed, Jimmy Page worked as a session musician in recording studios that required him to read music. During that time, he took a few classical guitar lessons to improve his music-reading skills. Classical music spans hundreds of years and thousands of composers, but two of the most famous composers are Beethoven and Bach. Beethoven's "Ode to Joy" is one of the most popular pieces of classical music, and Jimmy plays Bach's "Bouree in E Minor" during "Heartbreaker" on the live album *How the West Was Won*. You'll also learn a tune based on Bach's music on page 54.

ROCKABILLY SOUND Track 26

Power Chords

On page 18, you learned to play two notes together. Technically, a chord consists of three or more notes played together, but when you see chords with the symbols A5, D5, or E5 above them, they are special two-note chords called *power chords*. Power chords are some of the most important chords in rock. Add some distortion and play them loud, and you will see where they got their name.

THREE-CHORD PROGRESSION 🔊 Track 27

DOWN YOU GO 🔊 Track 28

This example is in the style of "Another One Bites the Dust" by Queen.

22

ROCK DUET

This song is a *duet*, which is a piece written for two performers. You can play either the first or second part. Have a teacher or friend accompany you. Do this with all of the duets in this book.

BOP THE BLITZ Track 30

This example is in the style of "Blitzkrieg Bop" by The Ramones.

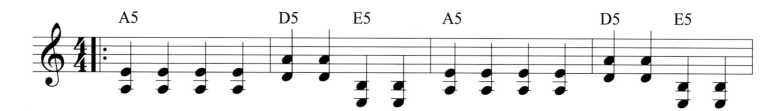

The Second String B 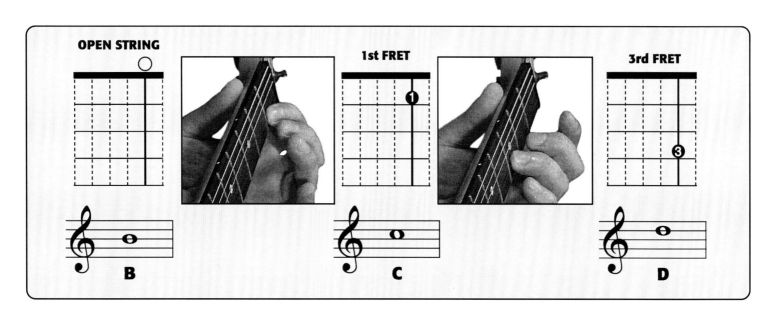 Track 31

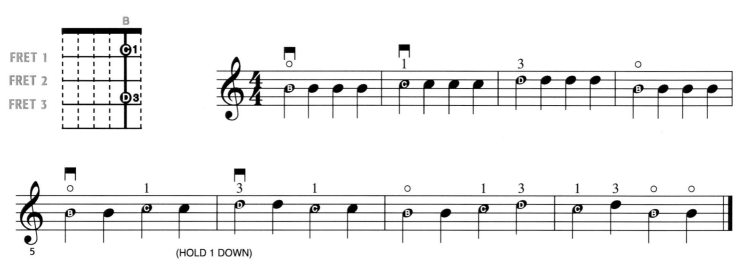

CLASSIC ROCK LICK  Track 32

FIVE-STRING ROCK  Track 33

SATISFYING LICK  Track 34

This example is in the style of "Satisfaction" by The Rolling Stones.

26

DON'T MISS THE TRAIN  Track 35

This is in the style of "Last Train to Clarksville" by the Monkees.

GIVE ME A HAND, LADY  Track 36

This is in the style of "Help Me Rhonda" by The Beach Boys.

ROCKIN' IN D  Track 37

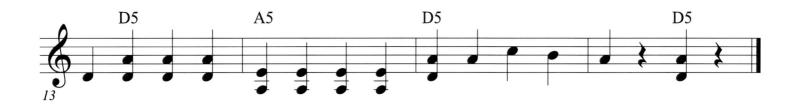

The First String E Track 38

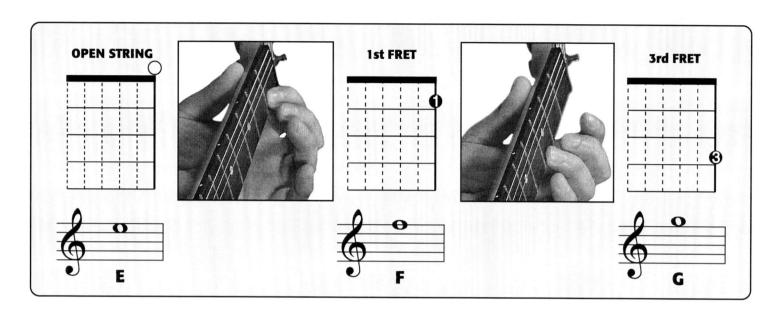

JAMMING WITH E, F, AND G Track 39

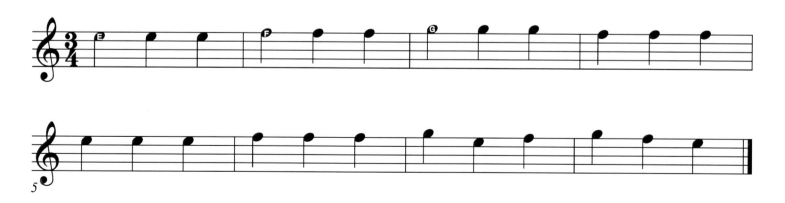

REVIEW

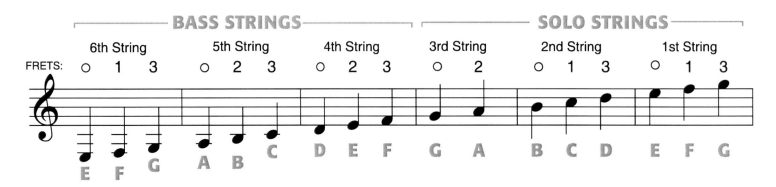

AURA LEE  Track 40

Elvis Presley recorded this folk song in a modern version called "Love Me Tender."

The Major Scale

A *major scale* is a specific pattern of eight tones in alphabetical order. The pattern of *whole steps* and *half steps* is what gives the major scale its distinct sound. The distance from one fret to the next fret, up or down, is a half step. Two half steps make a whole step.

whole step, whole step, half step, whole step, whole step, whole step, half step.

The highest note of the scale, having the same letter name as the first note, is called the *octave* note.

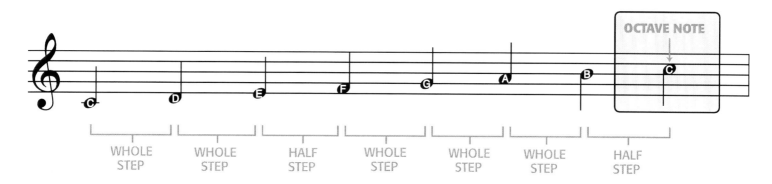

C Major Scale

It is easier to visualize whole steps and half steps on a piano keyboard. Notice there are whole steps between every note except E–F and B–C.

Whole steps - One key between

Half steps - No key between

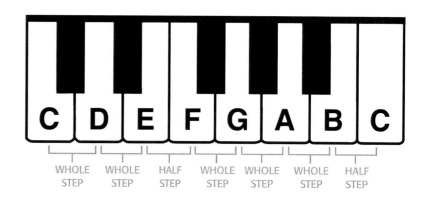

C MAJOR SCALE EXERCISE Track 41

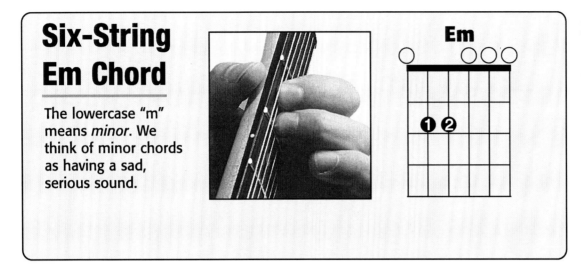

Six-String Em Chord

The lowercase "m" means *minor*. We think of minor chords as having a sad, serious sound.

A chord name like C, without an "m" after the letter name, indicates a *major* chord, which has a happier, brighter sound.

Place your 1st and 2nd fingers on the 5th and 4th strings and strum all six strings. This chord can also be played with your 2nd and 3rd fingers.

You learned to strum back on page 5. Since then, you have been strumming two-string power chords. On this page, you are going to be strumming a full six-string Em chord. The "m" in Em stands for "minor," so when you see "Em," you say "E Minor."

Quarter-Note Slash

Instead of using notes, sometimes chords are notated with slashes. A quarter-note slash tells you to play a chord for one beat. If there is more than one quarter-note slash in a row, the chord symbol above the first note is played for each slash. In this example, the Em chord is played four times.

Play four measures of the the Em chord. Count out loud and keep the rhythm even. Strum firmly and directly downward across the strings to produce a nice full sound.

EM STRUMMING EXERCISE Track 42

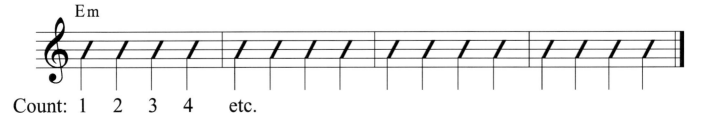

Count: 1   2   3   4   etc.

Five-String A⁷ Chord

 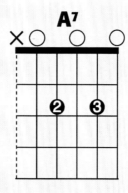

X or dashed line = Some sheet music will use an X to show a string not played, but other music will show a dashed line. This book uses both.

Place your 2nd and 3rd fingers on the 4th and 2nd strings, respectively, and only strum the 5th through 1st strings. Unlike the six-string Em chord, you do not strum the 6th string. Instead, you only strum starting on the 5th string.

The "7" in A⁷ stands for "seventh," so when you see "A⁷," you say either "A Seventh," or "A Seven."

Play four measures of the A⁷ chord. Count out loud and keep the rhythm even. Remember to strum firmly and directly downward across the strings to produce a nice full sound.

STRUMMING THE A⁷ CHORD Track 43

Count: 1 2 3 4 etc.

In this example, you are changing chords in each measure. Since both chords are played using the 2nd finger on the 4th string at the 2nd fret, you need only lift the 1st finger and place the 3rd finger. Play it slowly at first, and as you change chords, lift and place the two fingers smoothly and at exactly at the same time. Gradually increase the speed as you become more comfortable changing chords.

STRUMMING EM AND A⁷ CHORDS Track 44

MINOR TWO-CHORD ROCK 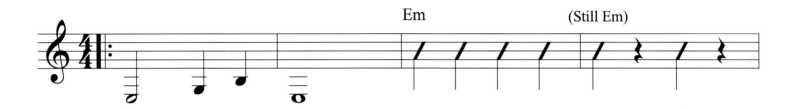 **Track 45**

This tune uses the two chords you know, along with single notes and rests. Even when there are rests, you continue to play the same chord until a new chord symbol is used. In the last two measures, you change quickly from Em to A7 and back. Practice just those two measures slowly until you can change chords in time, and then play the entire tune.

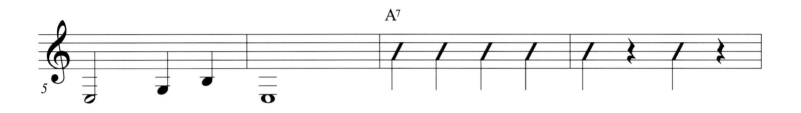

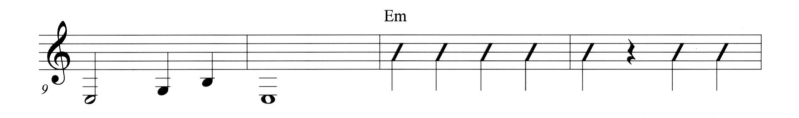

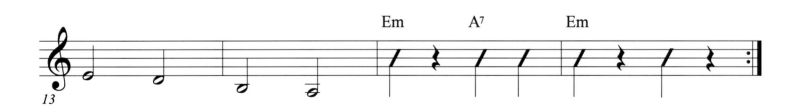

Introducing High A Track 46

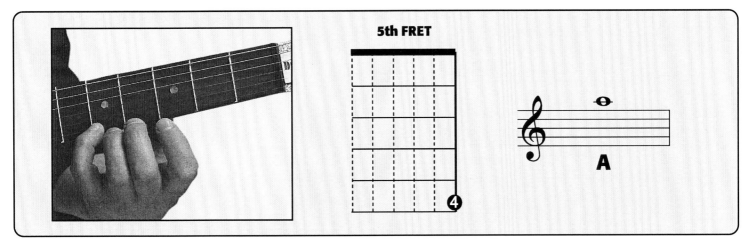

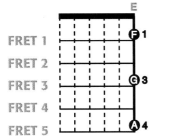

ROCKIN' IN DORIAN MODE Track 47

A *mode* is a type of scale that uses the notes of another scale, such as the major scale (page 29), in a different order. The *Dorian mode* uses the notes of the C major scale starting on D instead of C.

Ties

A *tie* is a curved line that connects two or more notes of the same pitch. When two notes are tied, the second one is not played; rather, the value is added to the first note.

Hold D for 5 beats.

RAINFOREST ROMP 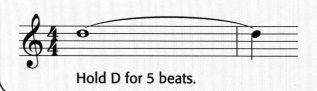 Track 48

This is in the style of "Welcome to the Jungle" by Guns N' Roses.

NICE ATTIRE Track 49

This is in the style of "Sharp Dressed Man" by ZZ Top.

Eighth Notes 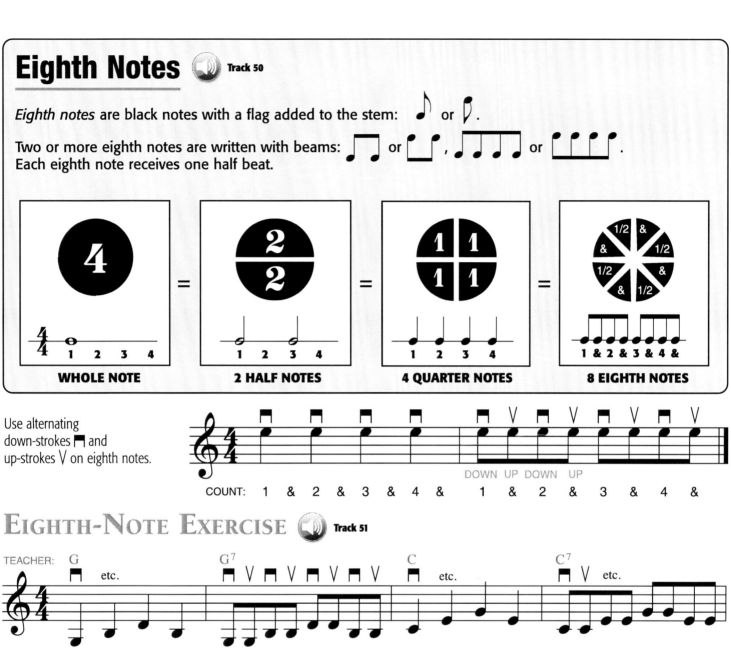 Track 50

Eighth notes are black notes with a flag added to the stem: ♪ or ♩.

Two or more eighth notes are written with beams. Each eighth note receives one half beat.

Use alternating down-strokes ⊓ and up-strokes V on eighth notes.

EIGHTH-NOTE EXERCISE Track 51

ELLIS ISLAND Track 52

This is in the style of "Immigrant Song" by Led Zeppelin.

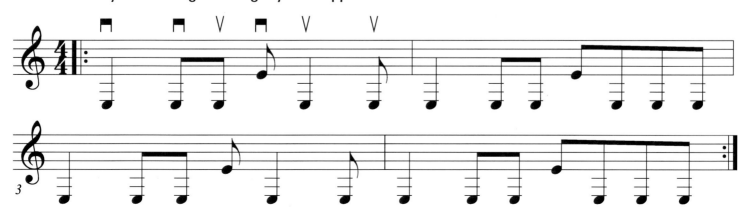

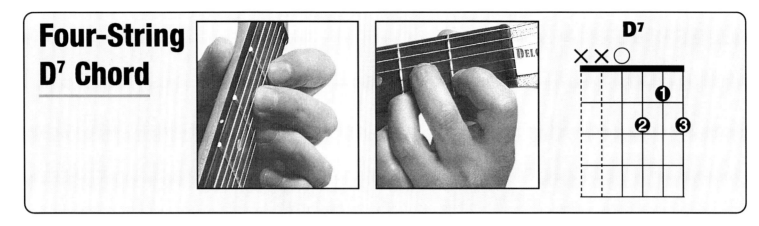

Four-String D⁷ Chord

This chord uses three fingers. Place your 1st finger on the 2nd string, 1st fret, and 2nd and 3rd fingers on the 3rd and 1st strings. Only strum the 4th through 1st strings. Do not strum the 5th or 6th strings.

Play four measures of the D⁷ chord. Count out loud and keep the rhythm even. Remember to strum firmly and directly downward across the strings to produce a nice full sound.

Track 53

D⁷

Count: 1 2 3 4 etc.

D⁷ AND A⁷ CHORD EXERCISE Track 54

Remember to practice the changes slowly, and then gradually increase the speed as you become more comfortable changing chords.

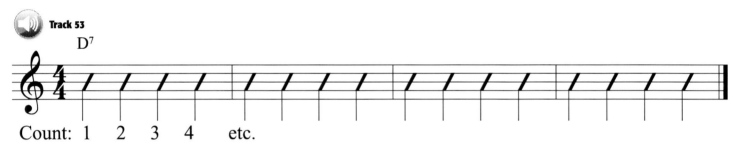

D⁷ CHORD WITH NOTES Track 55

This example combines the D⁷ chord with single notes.

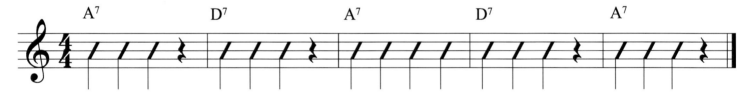

Six-String E Chord

 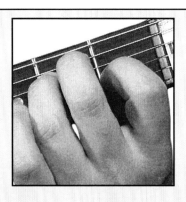 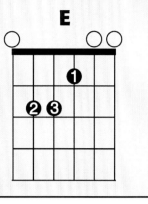

This chord uses three fingers. Place your 1st finger on the 3rd string, 1st fret, and 2nd and 3rd fingers on the 5th and 4th strings. Strum all six strings.

The six-string E chord is a major chord. When the chord name is just a letter, such as "E," it is called a major chord. Say "E Major." The E minor chord sounds dark or sad, but the E major chord sounds bright or happy.

Introducing the Eighth-Note Slash

Like an eighth note, the eighth-note slash lasts for one half beat. Two or more eighth-note slashes are written with beams.

EIGHTH-NOTE SLASH EXERCISE Track 56

This exercise uses the E and A⁷ chords with quarter- and eighth-note slashes.

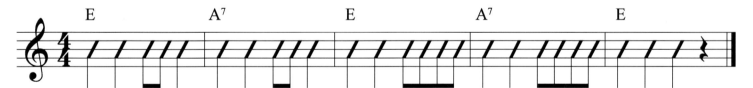

STRUMMING EXERCISE WITH E CHORD Track 57

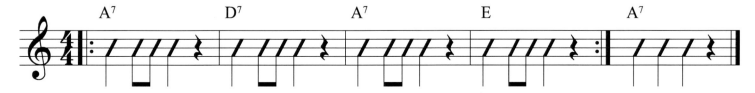

Five-String A Chord

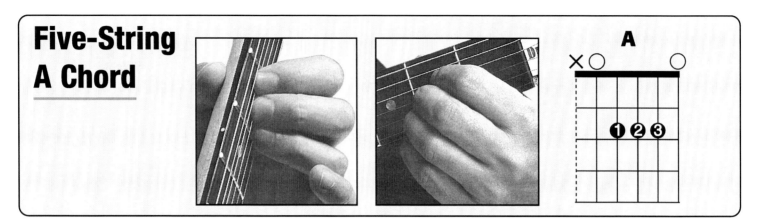

The five-string A major chord uses three fingers. Place your 1st, 2nd, and 3rd fingers on the 4th, 3rd, and 2nd strings at the 2nd fret. Strum the top five strings.

Remember to strum firmly and directly downward across the strings to produce a nice full sound.

Track 58

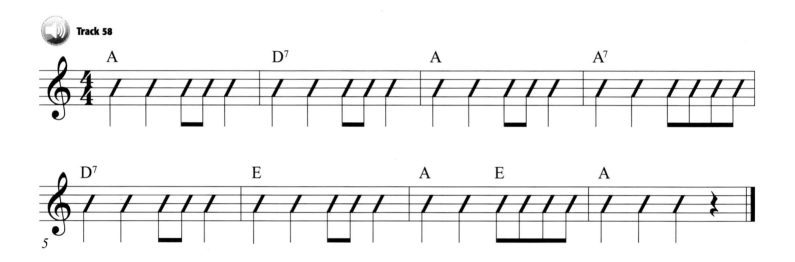

MINOR AND MAJOR **Track 59**

This example uses both the E and Em chords. Listen to how the mood changes when you play the major and minor chords.

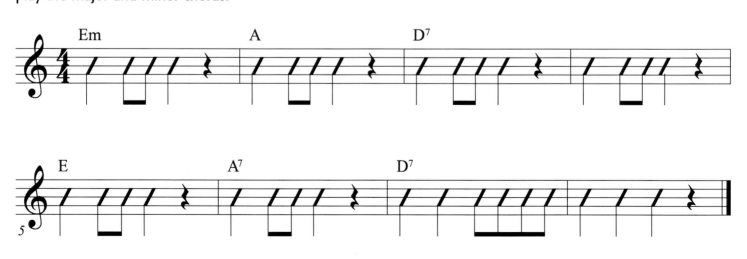

Vacate the Sky 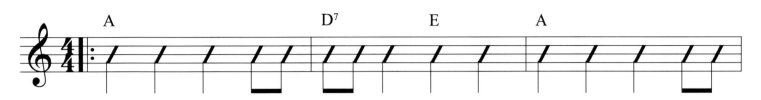 Track 60

This is in the style of "Get Off of My Cloud" by The Rolling Stones.

Doo Dah, Poo Bah 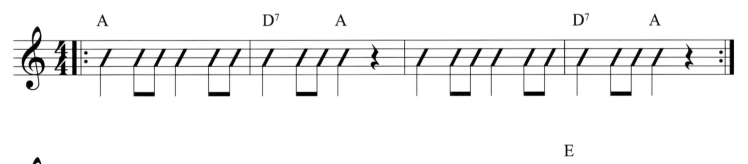 Track 61

This is in the style of "Do Wah Diddy Diddy" by Manfred Mann.

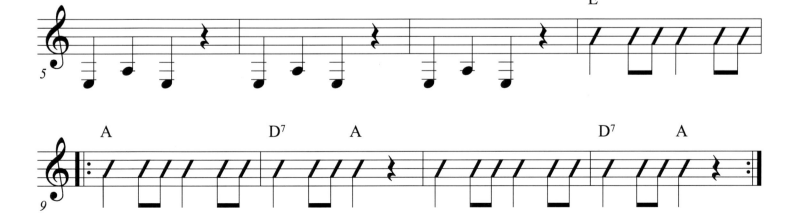

Eleven Classic Rock Strumming Patterns **Track 62**

These will work with any chord progression. Try E the first time through, and A the second time.

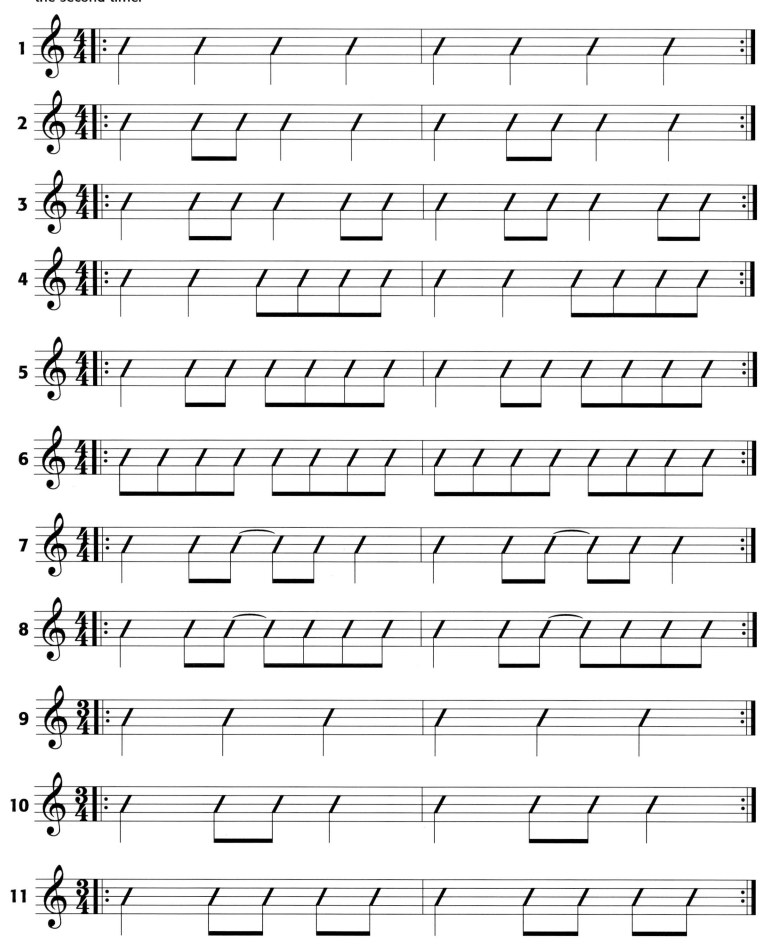

ROUGH EVENING Track 63

This is in the style of "Hard Day's Night" by The Beatles.

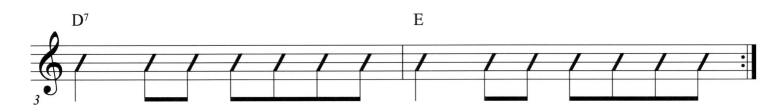

ALWAYS BEEN CRAZY Track 64

This is in the style of "Born to Be Wild" by Steppenwolf.

KEEP IT TO YOURSELF Track 65

This is in the style of "You've Got to Hide Your Love Away" by The Beatles. Eddie Vedder of Pearl Jam also recorded this song.

Sharps ♯, Flats ♭, and Naturals ♮

The C Major Scale (page 29) is created from half steps (one fret) and whole steps (two frets). Sharp ♯, flat ♭ and natural ♮ signs change the notes you already know.

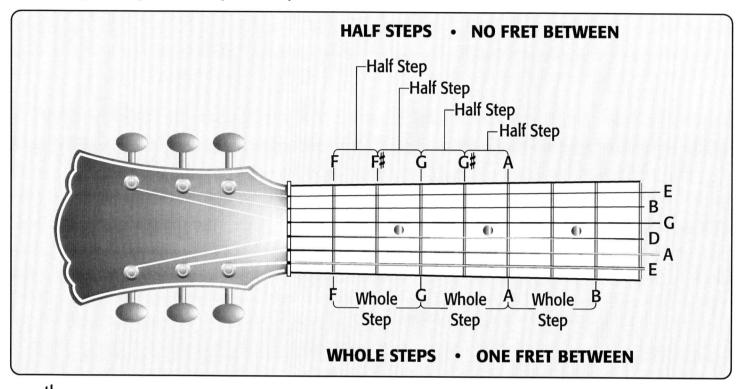

♯ SHARPS **raise** the note a half step. Play the next fret higher.

♭ FLATS **lower** the note a half step. If the note is fingered, play the next fret lower.

If the note is open, play the 4th fret of the next lower string—except if that string is **G** (3rd string), then play the 3rd fret.

♮ NATURALS **cancel** a previous sharp or flat.

When added within a measure, sharps, flats, and naturals are called *accidentals*. A bar line cancels a previous accidental in the measures that follow.

The Chromatic Scale Track 66

The *chromatic scale* is formed exclusively of half steps. The ascending chromatic scale uses sharps ♯. The descending chromatic scale uses flats ♭. Notes that have the same fingering but different names, like B♭ and A♯, are called *enharmonic equivalents*.

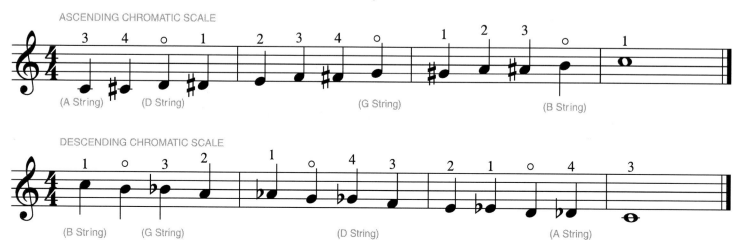

Before you play "Chromatic Rock," go back to page 29 and play the C major scale; then play the chromatic scale on page 42 and listen to the difference.

CHROMATIC ROCK Track 67

BLUESY ACCIDENTALS Track 68

WET DUET

Track 69.1 Full Performance
Track 69.2 Part 1
Track 69.3 Part 2

This is in the style of "Rain" by The Beatles.

45

Signs of Silence

Stop the sound of the strings by touching
them lightly with the heel of your hand.

♪	**EIGHTH REST**	= ½ COUNT
♩	**QUARTER REST**	= 1 COUNT
▬	**HALF REST**	= 2 COUNTS
▬	**WHOLE REST**	= 4 COUNTS IN $\frac{4}{4}$ TIME
		3 COUNTS IN $\frac{3}{4}$ TIME

TAKE A REST Track 70

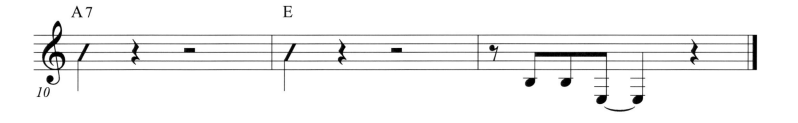

UGLY TIMES  Track 71

This is in the style of "Good Times Bad Times" by Led Zeppelin. You will be learning an authentic version of this song on page 62!

STOP-TIME BASS LINE  Track 72

Playing Two Notes Together: Blues Patterns

E Blues Boogie Track 73

Most of the rock music we hear is based on the blues. Much of the time, when you listen to some of the world's greatest rock guitarists—such as Eric Clapton, Jimi Hendrix, Jimmy Page, and John Mayer—you are really hearing the blues played loud with a rock beat.

Start by playing E5 using your 1st finger on the 2nd fret of the 5th string.

Keeping your 1st finger down, add your 3rd finger to the 4th fret of the 5th string to create E6.

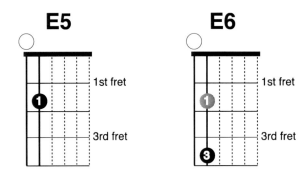

Now, go back and forth between these two shapes, and you are a blues-rock guitarist, too!

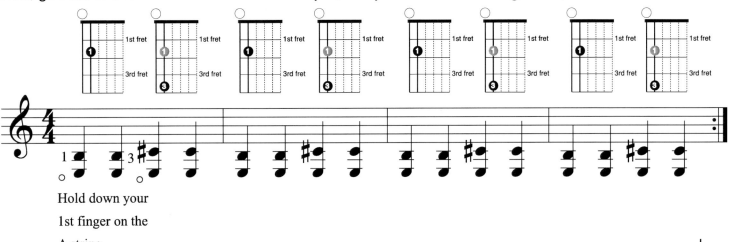

Hold down your

1st finger on the

A string

A Blues Boogie Track 74

The blues pattern on the 5th and 4th strings is just like the blues pattern built on the 6th and 5th strings (above). As with "E Blues Boogie," hold down your 1st finger on the D string throughout.

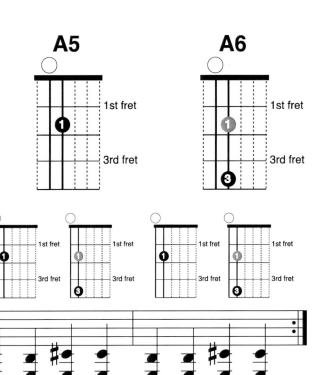

Move Up the Neck on the 6th String

The note on the 3rd fret of the 6th string is G. As you learned on page 8, the next note in the musical alphabet after G is A. Let's learn three more notes on the 6th string. All you have to do is move your left hand farther up the neck. A, B, and C are on the 5th, 7th, and 8th frets. You can play those three notes with either your 1st or 3rd finger, or even better, use both fingers, as shown in the diagram and photos below.

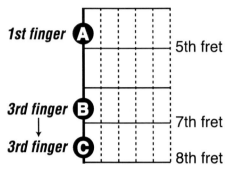

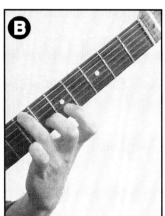

PRACTICE A, B, AND C **Track 75**

When your fingers move up the neck, you are changing *position*. Position refers to a four-fret area starting from where your 1st finger is located. For example, if your 1st finger is at the 1st fret, you are in *1st position*, if your 1st finger is at the 5th fret, you are in 5th position. In the example below, notice the fingering change on beat 2 of the second measure—this allows you to smoothly change to 5th position. The lines connecting the left-hand finger numbers show when you are shifting positions.

TWO POSITIONS ON THE 6TH STRING **Track 76**

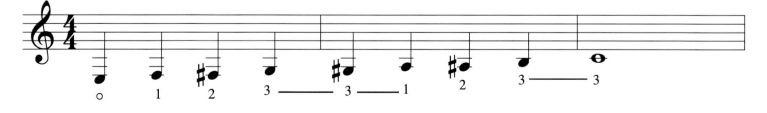

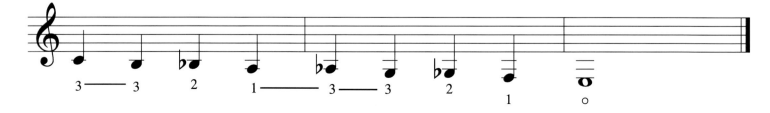

Move Up the Neck on the 5th String

Just as you did on the 6th string, you can move up the neck on the 5th string. And like the 6th string, the next notes in the alphabet—D, E, and F—fall on the 5th, 7th, and 8th frets.

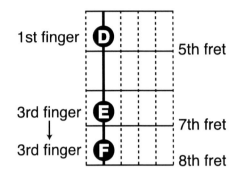

PRACTICE D, E, AND F Track 77

TWO POSITIONS ON THE 5TH STRING Track 78

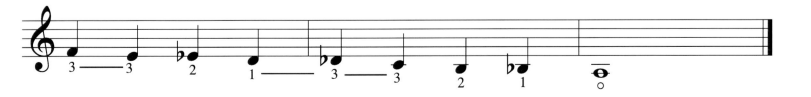

Move Up the Neck on the 4th String

Just as you did on the 5th and 6th strings, you can move up the neck on the 4th string. The next notes in the alphabet, G and A, fall on the 5th and 7th frets.

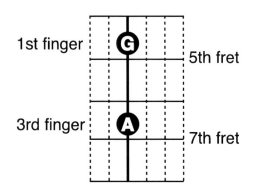

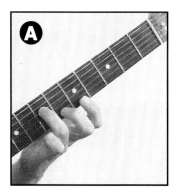

TWO POSITIONS ON THE 4TH STRING Track 79

Move Up the Neck on the 3rd String

Just as you did on the 4th, 5th, and 6th strings, you can move up the neck on the 3rd string. The next natural notes in the alphabet, C and D, fall on the 5th and 7th frets.

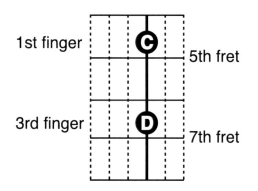
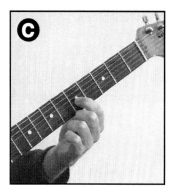
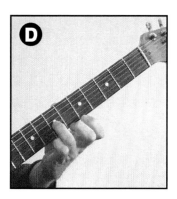

TWO POSITIONS ON THE 3RD STRING Track 80

CLASSIC ROCK LICK WITH 5S AND 7S Track 81

This is the same lick as Classic Rock Lick on page 24. This time, play the notes on just the 5th and 7th frets with your 1st and 3rd fingers.

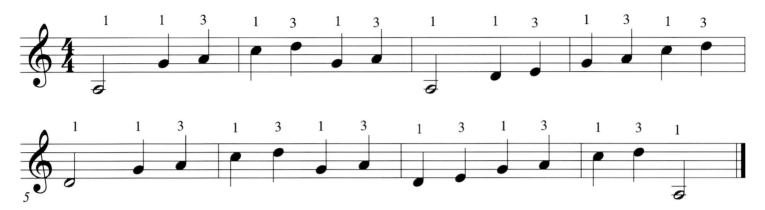

More On Power Chords

Since page 18, you have been playing two-note power chords. In a two-note power chord, the top note is five notes higher than the bottom note. In the case below, the bottom note is low E, so the top note is B.

E	F	G	A	B
1	2	3	4	5

This is why a power chord is often called a "5" chord. For example, the chord diagram on the right is a power chord built on E, so this is why we call it E5. The E6 chord you learned on page 47 has a top note six notes higher than the bottom note.

Now, try fingering this power chord using your 3rd finger on the B. You'll see why below.

E5

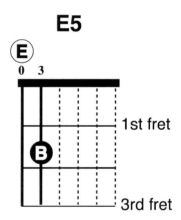

Power Chords Are Moveable

Try this: Slide your 3rd finger up one fret—from the 2nd to the 3rd fret of the 5th string—and add your 1st finger to F on the 1st fret of the 6th string. Play it!

Now, keep your fingers in their positions but shift up the neck so your 1st finger is on G at the 3rd fret of the 6th string, and your 3rd finger is on D on the 5th fret of the 5th string.

See? You can move this chord anywhere on these two strings and it will sound great! As you will see later, you can also move power chords on other strings.

F5

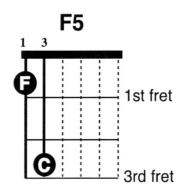

G5

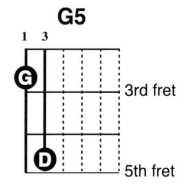

52

POWER CHORD ROCK Track 82

MORE POWER CHORD ROCK Track 83

"More Power Chord Rock" uses the most famous blues, rock, and jazz progression, the *12-bar blues*. This 12-measure song form is the basis for thousands of songs, and although it usually consists of only three chords, it can be played in many different ways. This example is a very basic way to play the 12-bar blues.

Count "1 & 2 & 3 & 4 &" throughout, and play on every count. Use your 1st finger on the 2nd fret, and 3rd finger on the 4th. Just be careful to strum the right strings, as some of the chords are on the 6th and 5th strings, and some of them are on the 5th and 4th. Have fun!

Six-String G Chord

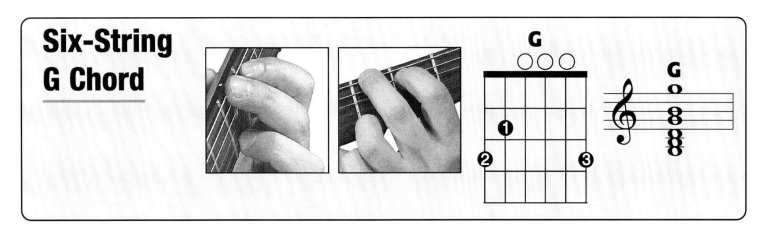

Chords in Standard Notation

If the G chord shown above feels too difficult, you can use this easier alternative four-string fingering:

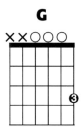

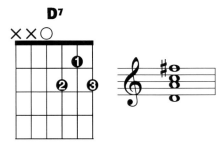
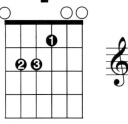

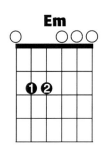
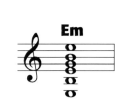

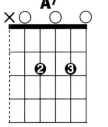

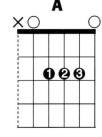

CHORDS IN NOTES Track 84

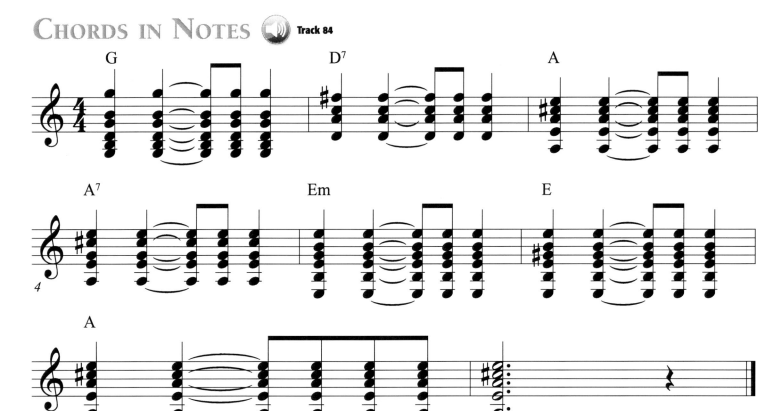

Rockin' the Bach  Track 85

Back on page 20, you learned the classical piece "Ode to Joy" by Beethoven. J. S. Bach was another classical composer who wrote memorable melodies that have inspired countless rock guitarists. His famous piece "Minuet in G," written in 1725, features a melody that is still used today in popular songs and movies. The original version of Minuet in G was written in $\frac{3}{4}$ time, but this arrangement is in $\frac{4}{4}$ to give it more of a rock feel.

Adapted from a Bach Minuet

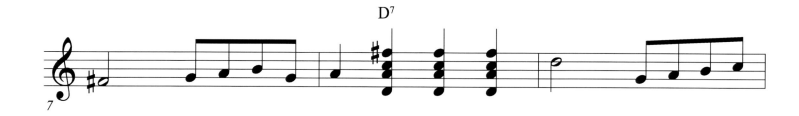

This next tune, in the style of The Beatles' "Birthday," uses accidentals and power chords with roots on three strings. Try fingering notes on the 4th fret with your pinky to reduce the motion of your right hand.

PARTY, PARTY  **Track 86**

Rock and Blues Licks and Tricks

ROCK LICK 1  Track 87

Here is a fun lick to play. Learn it and try turning it into your own rock song.

The Bend

This symbol ⌐ indicates a bend, which tells you to "pull" the fretted string down toward the floor. (Note: In some cases, you will "push" the string up toward the ceiling to achieve a bend.)

Keep your finger firmly on the string while doing this, and you'll be rewarded with a cool, bluesy bending sound. This is one way guitarists imitate a blues singer's voice, which will often glide from note to note. We can do little bends that add just a little bluesy character to a note, or we can do very big bends. BE CAREFUL...bending a note too far can break a string. To start sounding like Jimi Hendrix or Eric Clapton, try little blues bends on the following licks.

Low G before bend.

Bending low G.

ROCK LICK 1 WITH A BEND Track 88

ROCK LICK 2 Track 89

The E Minor Pentatonic Scale

The *pentatonic scale* has five notes, hence the name (*penta* is the Greek root for "five," think pentagon). Many rock and blues guitarists consider the E minor pentatonic scale one of the easiest tools for creating lead guitar solos.

The notes in the E minor pentatonic scale are: E G A B D. They are shown below on the 6th, 5th, and 4th strings. Play through them from the lowest note to the highest. It's a good idea to repeat the first note an octave higher at the end, as shown below.

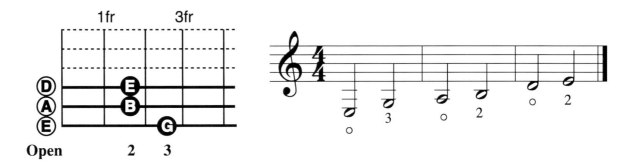

Following are some fun licks to play using this scale.

PENTATONIC LICK 1   Track 90

PENTATONIC LICK 2   Track 91

1950s BLUES ROCK TUNE  Track 92

When you bend the G on the 1st string, bend up towards the ceiling.

A Minor Pentatonic Scale

Let's learn the A minor pentatonic scale. Since this scale is focused on the note A, the A notes are gray in the diagram below.

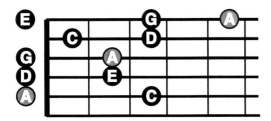

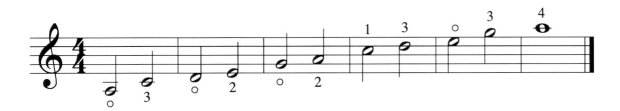

A MINOR PENTATONIC CALL AND RESPONSE Track 93

Many classic rock and blues licks use a style referred to as *call and response*, where one musical idea is stated and then is followed by a musical answer that ends the idea. Try this one.

Call

Response

Incomplete Measures or Pickups

Not every piece of music begins on beat 1. Sometimes, music begins with an incomplete measure called an *upbeat,* or *pickup.* If the pickup has just one beat, the last measure will have only three beats in $\frac{4}{4}$ or two beats in $\frac{3}{4}$.

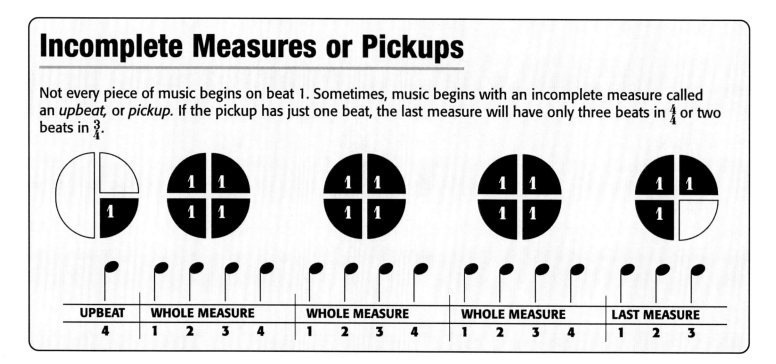

UPBEAT	WHOLE MEASURE				WHOLE MEASURE				WHOLE MEASURE				LAST MEASURE		
4	1	2	3	4	1	2	3	4	1	2	3	4	1	2	3

HOUSE OF THE RISING SUN Track 94

Eric Burdon and the Animals turned this traditional song into a rock hit in the 1960s. All the notes are from the A minor pentatonic scale.

* Try bending this note up by fingering it on the D string.

12-Bar Blues Duet

Track 95.1 Full Performance
Track 95.2 Part 1
Track 95.3 Part 2

Have a friend or teacher play the lower part while you rock out on this blues solo.

Good Times Bad Times (Intro) Track 96

Words and Music by
Jimmy Page, John Paul Jones,
and John Bonham

Guitar Fingerboard Chart
Frets 1–12

STRINGS

	6th	5th	4th	3rd	2nd	1st
	E	A	D	G	B	E

FRETS / **STRINGS**

Fret	6th	5th	4th	3rd	2nd	1st
Open	E	A	D	G	B	E
1st Fret	F	A#/B♭	D#/E♭	G#/A♭	C	F
2nd Fret	F#/G♭	B	E	A	C#/D♭	F#/G♭
3rd Fret	G	C	F	A#/B♭	D	G
4th Fret	G#/A♭	C#/D♭	F#/G♭	B	D#/E♭	G#/A♭
5th Fret	A	D	G	C	E	A
6th Fret	A#/B♭	D#/E♭	G#/A♭	C#/D♭	F	A#/B♭
7th Fret	B	E	A	D	F#/G♭	B
8th Fret	C	F	A#/B♭	D#/E♭	G	C
9th Fret	C#/D♭	F#/G♭	B	E	G#/A♭	C#/D♭
10th Fret	D	G	C	F	A	D
11th Fret	D#/E♭	G#/A♭	C#/D♭	F#/G♭	A#/B♭	D#/E♭
12th Fret	E	A	D	G	B	E

STRINGS (fingerboard diagram, left)

6th 5th 4th 3rd 2nd 1st
E A D G B E

Fret	6th	5th	4th	3rd	2nd	1st
1	F	A#/B♭	D#/E♭	G#/A♭	C	F
2	F#/G♭	B	E	A	C#/D♭	F#/G♭
3	G	C	F	A#/B♭	D	G
4	G#/A♭	C#/D♭	F#/G♭	B	D#/E♭	G#/A♭
5	A	D	G	C	E	A
6	A#/B♭	D#/E♭	G#/A♭	C#/D♭	F	A#/B♭
7	B	E	A	D	F#/G♭	B
8	C	F	A#/B♭	D#/E♭	G	C
9	C#/D♭	F#/G♭	B	E	G#/A♭	C#/D♭
10	D	G	C	F	A	D
11	D#/E♭	G#/A♭	C#/D♭	F#/G♭	A#/B♭	D#/E♭
12	E	A	D	G	B	E

CERTIFICATE OF PROMOTION

ALFRED'S BASIC
ROCK GUITAR METHOD

This certifies that

_____

has mastered
Alfred's Basic
Rock Guitar Method 1

Teacher _____

Date _____